BE A MAKER!

Maker Projects for Kids Who Love

PAPER ENGINEERING

REBECCA SJONGER

Crabtree Publishing Company
www.crabtreebooks.com

Crabtree Publishing Company

www.crabtreebooks.com

Author: Rebecca Sjonger

Series Research and Development: Reagan Miller

Editors: Sarah Eason, Harriet McGregor, Tim Cooke, and Philip Gebhardt

Proofreaders: Claudia Martin, Wendy Scavuzzo, and Petrice Custance

Editorial director: Kathy Middleton

Design: Paul Myerscough

Cover design: Paul Myerscough

Photo research: Rachel Blount

Production coordinator and Prepress technician: Tammy McGarr

Print coordinator: Katherine Berti

Consultant: Jennifer Turliuk, Bachelor of Commerce, Singularity University Graduate Studies Program at NASA Ames, Former President of MakerKids

Production coordinated by Calcium Creative

Photo Credits:

t=Top, bl=Bottom Left, br=Bottom Right

Valerie Heath: Tunnel book by Anna Clark, photo by Valerie Heath, Saint Francis of Assisi School, West Des Moines, Iowa: p. 7; Steve Messam: pp. 1, 15; Hawcock Books: p.19; Hyunjoo Oh: © 2015 HyunJoo Oh, All Rights Reserved: pp. 26–27; Robert Sabuda: robertsabuda.com: pp. 4, 16–17; Matthew Shlian: www.mattshlian.com: pp. 5, 11; Shutterstock: AnnaElizabeth Photography: p. 24; Bennyartist: p. 6; Exopixel: p. 14; Sergei Kardashev: p. 8; Yurchyks: p. 10; Tudor Photography: pp. 12–13, 18, 20–21, 28–29; Wikimedia Commons: Tokumeigakarinoaoshima: p. 22; Charles Young: www.paperholm.com: p. 23; Cybèle Young: cybeleyoung.ca: p. 9.

Cover: Tudor Photography

Library and Archives Canada Cataloguing in Publication

Sjonger, Rebecca, author
     Maker projects for kids who love paper engineering / Rebecca Sjonger.

(Be a maker!)
Includes index.
Issued in print and electronic formats.
ISBN 978-0-7787-2577-0 (hardback).--
ISBN 978-0-7787-2583-1 (paperback).--
ISBN 978-1-4271-1765-6 (html)

     1. Paper work--Juvenile literature. 2. Handicraft--Juvenile literature. I. Title.

TT870.S62 2016   j745.54   C2016-903331-7
                                         C2016-903332-5

Library of Congress Cataloging-in-Publication Data

Names: Sjonger, Rebecca, author.
Title: Maker projects for kids who love paper engineering / Rebecca Sjonger.
Description: St. Catharines, Ontario ; New York, New York : Crabtree Publishing Company, [2016] | Series: Be a maker! | Includes index.
Identifiers: LCCN 2016026031 (print) | LCCN 2016026374 (ebook) ISBN 9780778725770 (reinforced library binding) | ISBN 9780778725831 (pbk.) | ISBN 9781427117656 (Electronic HTML)
Subjects: LCSH: Paper work--Juvenile literature. | Handicraft--Juvenile literature. | Makerspaces--Juvenile literature.
Classification: LCC TT870 .S528 2016 (print) | LCC TT870 (ebook) | DDC 745.54--dc23
LC record available at https://lccn.loc.gov/2016026031

Crabtree Publishing Company

www.crabtreebooks.com   1-800-387-7650

Printed in Canada/072016/EF20160630

Published in Canada
Crabtree Publishing
616 Welland Ave.
St. Catharines, Ontario
L2M 5V6

Published in the United States
Crabtree Publishing
PMB 59051
350 Fifth Avenue, 59th Floor
New York, New York 10118

Published in the United Kingdom
Crabtree Publishing
Maritime House
Basin Road North, Hove
BN41 1WR

Published in Australia
Crabtree Publishing
3 Charles Street
Coburg North
VIC, 3058

CONTENTS

TIME TO MAKE!

How do simple sheets of paper transform into **three-dimensional** (3-D) objects? Makers get their hands on them! With a little creativity, there are almost no limits to what you can do with paper. Form it into a new shape by folding, rolling, or layering it. Carve a stack of paper into a one-of-a-kind sculpture. Design parts that pop up or move in other cool ways. Keep reading to explore **innovations**, or new ideas, in paper engineering and art. Get inspired and try it for yourself!

YOU CAN DO IT

Do you like to think "outside of the box" and experiment with the world around you? These skills are core to being a maker. Makers use their imaginations to find new ways of doing things. They take the lead in developing ideas. Original thinking pushes them to try things no one has considered before. Makers take risks and learn from their failures. They carry on until they discover solutions to problems. Put these skills together when you work with paper and you are on your way to making something amazing.

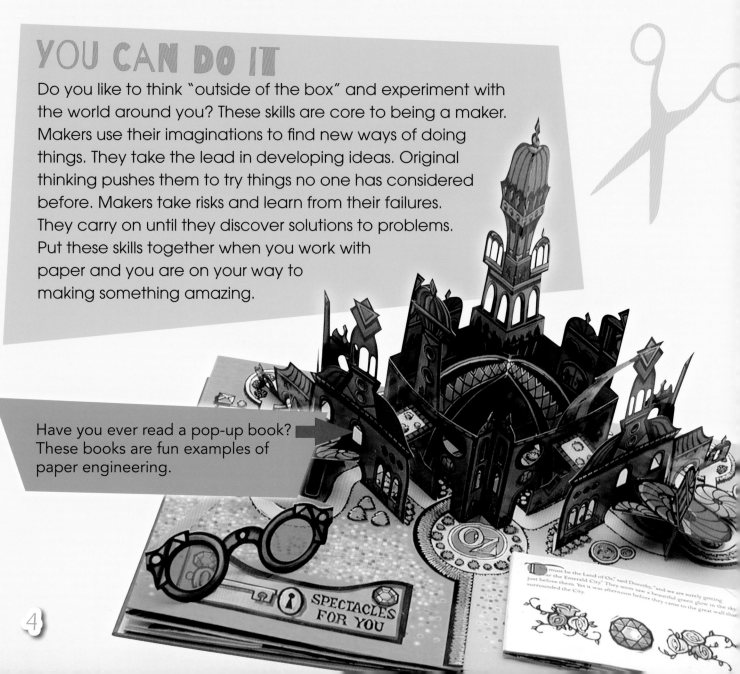

Have you ever read a pop-up book? These books are fun examples of paper engineering.

MAKER MOVEMENT

Paper engineering is a great activity for people who love art, technology, and math. The maker movement also includes many other areas of interest. The movement includes everything from woodworking to games and fashion design. Makers often look for ways to connect different fields. They might mix paper engineering with graphic design, for example. Maybe you will combine your own paper projects with **animation** (making stop-motion movies), photography, or other subjects. Join other makers by always keeping your mind open to new possibilities.

MAKE TOGETHER

Getting hands-on experience is essential for makers. **Makerspaces** allow makers to meet and **collaborate**. As makers work together, they communicate ideas and learn from one another. They share their dreams and their expertise. They may also share resources, such as materials and tools. Check with your local library or community center to see if they run a makerspace. You could also ask a teacher about starting one at your school. Another option is to try new ideas at home with friends and create your very own makerspace!

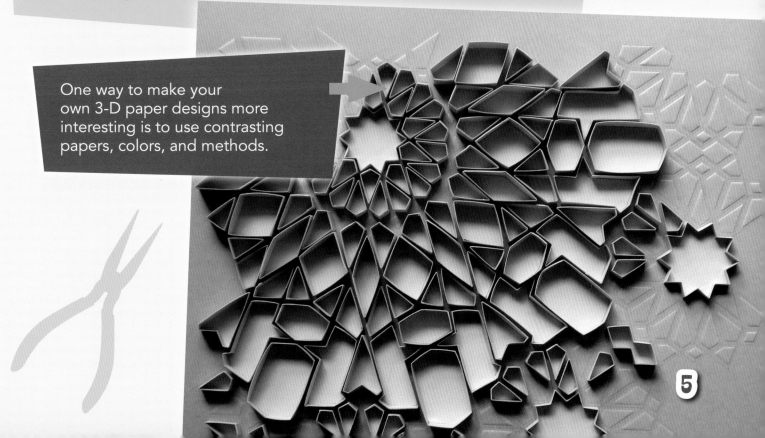

One way to make your own 3-D paper designs more interesting is to use contrasting papers, colors, and methods.

A LONG HISTORY

Chinese inventors created paper more than 2,000 years ago. They spread a **pulp** made of mashed hemp plants and water over a woven cloth. The pulp dried, and became a sheet of rough paper. Papermaking continued to develop in China over centuries. In the 4th century, papermaking spread across Asia. Each region experimented with its own materials and methods. When paper reached Europe in the 10th century, it was rare and valuable. Paper became widespread after Johannes Gutenberg created the printing press around 1440.

EARLY PAPER ART

Have you ever seen an **origami** crane? This kind of paper folding goes back to the 6th century in Japan. Origami started appearing soon after paper arrived in Japan. Paper was expensive. People saved it to make origami for important events such as weddings.

Older Chinese paper folding may have inspired origami. It is difficult to know for sure, since most ancient paper has broken down into pieces over time. Another ancient art form from China is paper cutting. People cut **intricate** designs from paper to create an image. It is still a **traditional** part of Chinese culture.

Origami, such as this crane, begins with a flat, square sheet of colored paper. A series of folds creates the 3-D object.

EUROPEAN PAPER ENGINEERING

Paper engineering began appearing in Europe with handmade **volvelles** in the 1200s. Volvelles are two or more paper wheels that users turn to combine different sets of **data**. They had various uses, including making calculations and tracking the Moon as it seemed to grow and shrink. Tabs, flaps, and pop-ups were other early movable parts. They were usually found in instruction books.

Paper engineering for entertainment came later. Pop-up books for children were not made until the 1800s. Tunnel books also became popular around that time. Tunnel books featured layered cutout designs. Accordion-folded paper sides held each sheet apart. Viewed from the front, they created a scene that appeared to be 3-D.

This modern tunnel book has the traditional accordion-folded sides. More complex tunnel books have many layers.

Be a Maker!

Early examples of paper engineering had clear functions, or purposes. For example, some medical books used moving parts to reveal the insides of the human body. Their makers educated people by using innovative designs. How does an object's function affect its form or appearance?

GLUE, PAPER, SCISSORS

Makers who work with paper often have a favorite kind of paper that they use. In some cases, the weight of the paper is important to a design. Compare tissue paper and construction paper, for example. They fold, shape, and move in different ways. Makers experiment with a variety of paper textures, too. They also consider the sizes in which paper is available. Many kinds of paper are available at office and art supply stores. For your projects, start by looking around your home for paper you can use or recycle.

Look around your home for supplies—you may already have most of the basics!

FOLDERS AND CUTTERS

Many makers use folders to crease paper. These long, flat tools are made of plastic or bone. You could use a very dull knife instead. The tip of a dried-up pen can **score**, or indent, paper. Cutting tools are helpful. Sharp scissors will get you started. You could also use a craft knife and a mat on which to cut. For safety, always pull the blade away from your body. Avoid paper cuts by being careful not to drag your fingers along the edges of paper.

IN YOUR TOOLBOX

Work with pencils, erasers, and art supplies that will not damage your paper. Find a white, water-based liquid glue. It should dry clear and quickly. Apply small amounts with a toothpick or paintbrush. Not using too much glue will help keep paper from wrinkling. Clothespins and paperclips can hold paper parts together as they dry.

Search through your school supplies for rulers and protractors. These tools allow you to make precise measurements. You could also use computer programs to help you create **templates**, or patterns. First, you plan, measure, and finalize your project onscreen. Next, you print your design and put it together.

Maker Cybèle Young formed each of these undersea artworks from colored Japanese paper.

Makers and Shakers

Cybèle Young

Canadian Cybèle Young (born 1972) makes complex paper sculptures. Many of her sculptures are miniature versions of everyday items. Some of her works have hundreds of layers of tiny pieces of paper. Young's playful art is the product of her imagination and a few simple supplies. The Japanese papers she uses look delicate, but they are strong. Her small set of tools includes scissors, craft knives, and needles.

9

REAMS OF POSSIBILITIES

Makers who work with paper rarely start a new project without first making a plan. They sketch concepts and imagine fresh ways of working with paper. They carefully measure each part before they begin to transform the paper. This is also a great time to collaborate with other makers. They often share suggestions and solutions that improve designs. Testing materials and exploring methods help makers decide what to make.

Simple rolls and folds can create amazing artworks! The colors you choose also have a big impact.

BOUNDLESS OPTIONS

How many ways can you think of to change the shape of paper? Consider what your fingers can do. They could tear, fold, or crumple paper. They can roll it into cones or twist it around a pencil. What happens when you use some of the tools described on the previous pages? Scissors cut paper to create different looks. But they can also be pulled down paper to curl it. A folder is meant for scoring paper or making sharp creases in it, but you can find other uses for it, too. A sharp tip could become a way to make holes.

SHAPE UP

Paper engineering becomes more complex when you use more than one piece of paper. Study the ways different makers construct with paper. How do they use it "behind the scenes" to make other parts pop up or move? Analyze their designs to help spark your own ideas.

One way to experiment with paper is to layer it. Customize each piece before putting them together. Think about the sizes, textures, and colors of the papers in your design. Form new shapes by gluing, stitching, or stapling paper together. Test your ideas by attaching paper with low-tack tape. The tape does not leave a sticky film behind and does not damage the paper when you pull it off.

Makers also shape paper using high-tech options. Some 3-D printers glue many layers of paper together then cut them based on a computer design. This creates some amazing 3-D objects.

Artist Matt Shlian planned ahead to ensure this project turned out perfectly. He named the artwork *Swire*.

Be a Maker!

Planning is key to the success of paper-engineering designs. What do you predict might happen if a maker skipped this stage? How would you start planning your own design project? Talk with friends about how you would plan a project as a group.

MAKE IT!
PAPER TUNNEL BOOK

Join centuries of makers by creating your own paper tunnel book! You can flip back to page 7 to see an example.

You can flip back to page 7 to see an example.

YOU WILL NEED
- A selection of colored, black, and white construction paper
- Glue or double-sided tape
- Craft knife
- Cutting mat
- Ruler
- Pencil
- Decorations

1
- Plan your design. It is a good idea to try it out using scrap paper first.

2
- Cut a sheet of construction paper in two halves, each 12 inches (30.5 cm) by 4½ inches (11.5 cm). Starting at the same end of the paper, mark seven 1-inch (2.5 cm) intervals along the edges of both of the long sides. Score lines between each pair of marks parallel to the end of the paper.
- Fold along your scored lines to achieve an accordion or fan effect.

3
- Take four pieces of colored construction paper 4 inches (10 cm) wide and 4½ inches (11.5 cm) high. Mark a 1-inch (2.5 cm) margin along both long sides and a ½-inch (1.25 cm) margin along both short sides. Draw your designs inside these margins on three of the pieces. (The 4th piece will be your background.)
- Using a craft knife and a cutting mat, cut away your designs on pieces 1 to 3.

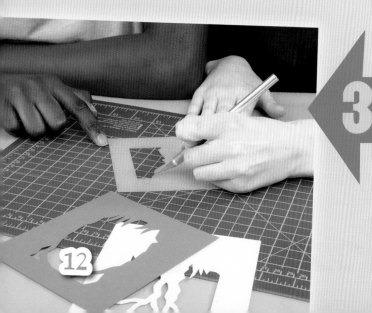

4 ● Glue or tape the background piece of construction paper (piece 4) to the last accordion fold on both sheets of paper, so that it joins the sheets of paper together.

5 ● Glue or tape pieces 1–3 into position between the sheets of paper, with one piece in each accordion fold.
● Add any decorations you choose to the inside and outside of the cover.

CONCLUSION

How does your tunnel book look when you view it from the front? Do the layers work together in the way you planned? If not, learn from your mistakes! You could also ask your friends for their feedback on your book.

Make It Even Better!

Examine your finished tunnel book. Consider ways to build on it or improve it. For example, are there alternatives to the accordion sides? What other approaches could you try for holding up the pieces of construction paper?

3-D MASTERPIECES

People who work with paper are inventive and resourceful. They all start with similar materials, but they end up with countless designs. The same paper could become layered paper feathers or **papier-mâché** flowers. Here are just a few examples of the diverse things makers are doing with paper.

SMART CUTS

Calvin Nicholls brings drawings to life in his studio in Canada. He begins by making a pattern, which he cuts out and shapes onto a larger paper background. His 3-D animals are incredibly realistic, even when he uses nothing but white paper.

Su Blackwell carves and shapes pages from books. This British artist often creates fairy tale scenes. She sculpts text-covered paper into people, trees, and other objects. They rise up to create a scene from the book's opened and cut pages.

PAPER IN MOTION

Chinese maker Li Hongbo starts his designs by layering thousands of sheets of white paper. He glues each lightweight sheet together in a way that creates a bendable block. Then he carves the stack into a shape, such as a human head. The completed sculptures can be stretched out then returned to their original shapes.

Papier-mâché uses cheap paper such as newspaper or paper towels. Water mixed with glue or flour coats the paper so that it hardens as it dries.

Paper designs can also move in more dramatic ways. Have you ever seen or made a **mobile**? Wind blows the hanging pieces. **Geometric** 3-D paper shapes and origami are great choices for mobiles because each side looks interesting. Creating mobiles with paper parts is a great place for young makers to get their start!

PAPER WITH A PURPOSE

Some makers play with function in their designs. We all know that paper is made from wood, and some bridges are made from wood. Do you think that means a usable bridge could be built from paper? Steve Messam did just that in real life! He formed more than 20,000 sheets of red paper into an arch that could hold a person.

To make his bridge strong, Steve Messam made it an arch, which is a shape that adds support in bridge construction.

Be a Maker!

Each of these makers uses different kinds of paper. Your first projects may use recycled or printer paper. These papers are inexpensive but they are also delicate. What are some of the other pros and cons of different types of paper?

POP-UP PAPER

Have you ever pulled a tab, lifted a flap, or opened a pop-up in a picture book? When people talk about paper engineering, they usually mean movable parts like these. Pulling a tab causes part of a design to move. Flaps lift to reveal words or pictures. These devices allow readers to interact with a design. Pop-ups are often surprise elements. As the name suggests, these parts pop up from a page or artwork. They make paper engineering fun!

DESIGNS THAT POP

Greeting cards often contain simple pop-ups. When someone opens the card, a paper design "jumps out." The same kinds of pop-ups are also found in books. They activate when someone opens the pages to which the pop-ups are attached. One book can contain many pop-ups. There might even be more than one pop-up on a **spread** of two pages. Makers use a variety of cuts and folds to cause pop-ups to move in different ways. Flip to pages 18 and 19 to learn how to make your own basic pop-ups.

Count the pop-up elements on these pages of *Alice's Adventures in Wonderland* designed by Robert Sabuda.

POP-UP POWER

Cards and books are not the only places to find pop-ups. Makers experiment with pop-up techniques and use them to create 3-D sculptures. Unlike traditional pop-up cards and books, these artworks stay "popped up" all the time.

One style of pop-up art is called paper architecture because it focuses on buildings. There are rarely any added-on parts. Instead, makers usually cut and fold a single sheet of paper to create a pop-up structure. To see inspiring examples of paper architecture, run an Internet search for the Dutch artist Ingrid Siliakus.

Robert Sabuda uses simple supplies to create cool, complex pop-ups.

Makers and Shakers

Matthew Reinhart and Robert Sabuda

Matthew Reinhart (born 1971) is an American pop-up star. He got his start after a chance meeting with Robert Sabuda (born 1965). Sabuda is another famous pop-up bookmaker and book illustrator. Sabuda inspired Reinhart to go to design school. Later, they collaborated on many pop-up books. Together they created the popular *Encyclopedia Prehistorica* and *Encyclopedia Mythologica* series. Dinosaurs, sea monsters, and magical creatures pop out of their pages. These illustrated pop-ups entertain, but they also educate, just like the earliest pop-up books.

MASTER THE MECHANICS

Pop-up designs may look wildly different, but they usually have two things in common. They often use stiff, heavy paper called card stock. It is smoother and thicker than construction paper. Card stock folds well and can hold a shape. It does not rip as easily as most other kinds of paper. Pop-ups also use behind-the-scenes constructions and layers.

FOLD AND CUT

Grab any sheet of paper and try making a basic pop-up layer. Fold the sheet in half by lining up the short ends. Starting in the middle of the fold, and parallel to the edge of the paper, draw two lines that are about three thumb-widths apart. Next, starting at the fold, cut one third of the way along both lines. Unfold the paper and push up the cut middle section to create a pop-up box. Finish the pop-up by sticking anything you want to the pop-up box. Adding an outer piece of folded paper will cover the hole at the back. Once you have the hang of it, try it with card stock.

You can also make a pop-up box by cutting out a small paper rectangle and folding it in half. Next, fold tabs at either end and glue them onto a larger sheet of folded paper to form a box. This method does not leave a hole in the back of your outer sheet of folded paper.

If you follow the "fold and cut" instructions above, your pop-up box will look similar to the example shown here.

PLAYING WITH POP-UPS

Once you master making one pop-up on a page, the next step is to add more pop-ups. Try making two or more box layers on one fold. Consider how anything you attach to the boxes will interact when the paper opens.

Experiment with shapes other than boxes. The shapes can be cut from or glued onto the folded paper. Some shapes can become part of the design, instead of just being building layers. Why not work with your friends as a team? Try five ideas and see which one works best.

Study these pop-up layers and attached images. How do tabs help this construction?

Be a Maker!

Makers need to be innovators who are willing to risk failure. Instead of finding setbacks discouraging, innovators try to learn from them. Have you ever learned something after a project did not go as planned? Can you think of some ways to deal with plans that do not work out? Share thoughts with your teammates.

MAKE IT!
MAKE IT POP

Use what you have learned about pop-ups to make your own greeting card. Challenge yourself to be truly creative, and design something you have never seen before.

YOU WILL NEED
- A selection of colored heavy-weight cards
- Glue or double-sided tape
- Craft knife
- Cutting mat
- Ruler
- Pencil
- Decorations

1

- Plan your design. It is a good idea to try it out using scrap paper first.
- Fold a piece of card in half by lightly folding it, then scoring it.
- Measuring along the fold, mark three evenly spaced tabs, each 1-inch (2.5 cm) wide. Draw two 5-inch (12.5 cm) lines for the first tab, two 3-inch (7.5 cm) lines for the next tab, and two 1-inch (2.5 cm) lines for the last tab. Cut along those lines, and score a line between the ends of the cuts on each tab.

- Open up the card and push the tabs through. You should have three steps inside your card.

2

3
- Cut out letters to spell H-I-!. Try them to make sure they are not too big. Temporarily attach them to the steps, then gently close the card. You should not be able to see them when the card is shut.

4
- Once you are happy with the letters, glue or tape them onto each step. Gently close and open the card to check positioning, then keep the card open for the glue to dry.
- Add more decorations.

CONCLUSION

Find or make your own envelope to go with your pop-up card. Who is the lucky person who will receive it? You can always make more! The extra practice will help you to perfect your pop-up mechanics.

Make It Even Better!

Assess your pop-up creation. Do you see any ways to improve it? What might happen if you combined multiple pop-up layers? Could you cut more steps to spell longer words?

MODELS AND MORE

Have you ever played with a paper model or toy? One of the most common is a paper airplane. Model planes have different designs and are put together in different ways. They are just one of many kinds of transportation that can be made into paper models. Other common paper models include buildings, animals, and cool geometric shapes. Some makers call these 3-D objects papercraft. Any object can have a paper version. Papercraft can also be original creations. Makers may decorate them or leave the paper plain.

MOVABLE PARTS

Some paper models include movable parts. These moving pieces go beyond flaps, tabs, and pop-ups. They include sliding panels, rotating pieces, and parts moved by **gears** and **cranks**. Makers often build these parts from paper. They may also use toothpicks, paper clips, nails, and other materials. Find out more about paper model construction on pages 24–25.

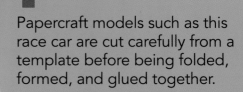

Papercraft models such as this race car are cut carefully from a template before being folded, formed, and glued together.

This structure and vehicle are examples of the Paperholm village created by Charles Young.

Charles Young's Paperholm project is a great example of a movable paper model. This Scotland-based maker creates a new paper model each day. Using white watercolor paper, he makes a huge variety of buildings, vehicles, and animals. Garage doors, cranes, and windmills are just some of the moving models in the village of Paperholm. See them for yourself at www. paperholm.com.

TEST MODELS

A prototype is the first model built to test a new design. Makers use them in many fields, including interior design and game-making. Paper is an inexpensive material that can be recycled. This makes it a great choice for prototypes that have many rounds of testing and improving. Sturdy papers such as cardboard and card stock hold up well to testing. Using different colors of paper can help show the different parts of a prototype.

Be a Maker!

Papercraft designs may look different, but their materials and building methods are often alike. Why do you think most paper models and toys use similar paper and construction methods? Discuss with friends how to make a paper model stand out from the crowd.

MODEL MAKING

Making a paper model or toy takes a lot of creativity—and a lot of planning. The process starts with **brainstorming** and sketching ideas. Next comes creating a template. Each piece is drawn on a flat sheet of paper. The measurements must be exact so that the parts fit together. The pattern shows lines for cutting and folding. Dotted lines often show where to fold, and solid lines show where to cut.

SHARING TEMPLATES

Fans of the video game *Minecraft* may have already tried making papercraft. *Minecraft* players share templates for 3-D paper versions of the game's elements. They collaborate online at websites such as PixelPaperCraft (www.pixelpapercraft.com). Even if you are not familiar with *Minecraft,* exploring these patterns can be helpful. Photos of finished projects show what each template creates. Most of the designs include building instructions and tips. You can use the basic ideas to help you with your own plans.

PAPER PARTS

For model making, choose a paper that is strong enough for building, but thin enough to fold and glue easily. Finding the right paper may take a few test runs. Note that many templates include the shapes and locations of tabs. These tabs tuck under other parts of the design.

This *Minecraft* design will become a paper model. Graph paper is helpful for measuring during the planning stage.

They provide a place to glue or tape the parts together. You can use the cube template on this page to get a feel for putting together a template with tabs. It could also be a starting point for your own creations.

Adding moving parts is another great way to customize a project. Parts can be something as simple as a piece that spins on a toothpick stuck into the model. For a bigger challenge, research how connected gears work together to power movement. Some makers even construct gears made from paper. These complex models involve a lot of planning, cutting, and folding. Start with simple models and work up to complex designs such as gears.

Copy this template onto a sheet of paper and try putting it together. You could turn your cube into a die, a house, or something entirely new!

Be a Maker!

Figuring out how to put together paper models requires imagination and problem solving. How many creative ways can you think of to join the parts of a design? What are the advantages and disadvantages of each idea? Share your thoughts with other makers and discuss as a group what you might do to improve your designs.

PAPER MEETS THE FUTURE

Traditional paper engineering combined with art does amazing things with little more than paper. However, some makers dream up ways to pair paper with more modern materials. Some of them experiment by adding mechanical, electronic, and computer parts to their paper creations. Paper **mechatronics** is the name of a new field in which technology, engineering, and art meet. The high-tech designs respond to their environments—they may begin to dance when a light shines on them!

SYSTEM SETUP

Paper mechatronic designs are systems in which connected parts work together. Most projects include computer controls, electronics, and mechanisms. They have **sensors** that collect data and send it to a small computer called a **microcontroller**. Its programming examines the data and sends instructions to **motors**. They cause various parts of the design to move. These components are often sold as kits. Usually, parts can be re used in later projects. The construction materials are often inexpensive, such as recycled cereal boxes.

Paper mechatronic projects include a variety of moving parts and motors.

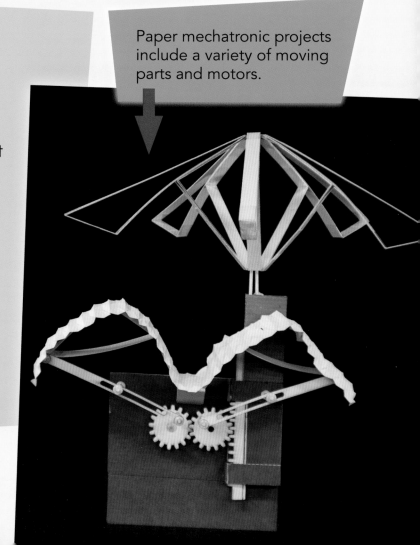

THE DESIGN PROCESS

Paper mechatronics creations begin with brainstorming ideas. Makers develop their ideas with sketches and computer design software. They figure out all the parts of the design. They then create a template, which is the pattern for the actual object. The model is built, tested, and improved until it works as well as it possibly can. At first, the moving parts may be human-operated. After these parts are tested, the designer adds electronics, microcontrollers, and motors to power and move the object. When the design is optimized, makers can share it with other makers.

HyunJoo Oh is a curious and talented maker in the new field of paper mechatronics.

Makers and Shakers

HyunJoo Oh

HyunJoo Oh (born 1984) earned degrees in fine arts and design at university in South Korea. Her passion for interactive artwork brought her to the United States, where she continued her studies. When a teacher showed her an innovative 3-D design, Oh was inspired to develop her own projects that combined art and technology. Now this paper mechatronics inventor shares her designs to encourage other makers. Check them out at www.ohhyunjoo.com.

MAKE IT!
CREATIVE CUBE STORAGE SYSTEM

Dream it, then build it! Starting with a basic paper cube, design a multi-part storage unit. Why not collaborate with a friend on this fun cube project?

YOU WILL NEED
- A selection of colored heavy-weight card stock
- Glue or double-sided tape
- Craft knife
- Cutting mat
- Ruler
- Pencil
- Paper fasteners
- Decorations

1

- Plan your design. Perhaps try it using scrap paper first.

2

- Make up a set of nine boxes based on the template on page 25. Cut them out carefully. Score the folds and tabs using a blunt edge, such as the tip of a dried-up pen, so they are easier to fold. Secure the bottom and sides using double-sided tape. Leave the lids open.

- Find the center of each lid and push a paper fastener through. This will act as a handle to open the box. It will also remind you which face of the box is the top! Open the paper fastener to hold it in place.

3

4

- Glue or tape the boxes together to form a storage unit.

CONCLUSION

Using similar materials and methods, you could create mobiles, sculptures, or models. What other projects could you make by combining several paper cubes? Remember, the only limit is your imagination!

Make It Even Better!

How could you improve your project? What would happen if you added more than one layer of storage cubes? How would you make them sturdy and accessible?

GLOSSARY

animation A kind of movie-making in which the appearance of movement is created by slightly moving nonliving objects in each frame

brainstorming Coming up with as many ideas as possible

collaborate Work together toward a common goal

cranks Parts of a machine that have a handle, which is turned to move another part

data Facts or information

gears Wheel-shaped machine parts with teeth that connect with and move other gears

geometric A word describing square, rectangle, and circle shapes

innovations Things that are newly introduced, such as ideas, methods, or devices

intricate Complicated and detailed

makerspaces Places where makers gather to innovate, share resources, and learn from one another

mechatronics A technology that combines electrical, mechanical, and systems engineering

microcontroller A tiny computer that controls the operation of a device

mobile A hanging decorative structure that moves freely in the air

motors Machines that produce motion

origami Japanese-style paper folding that uses square sheets of paper

papier-mâché A mixture of paper and glue that becomes hard when dry

pulp A damp, soft substance made from mixing natural materials and water together

score To make a light indent in something such as paper

sensors Devices that detect events or changes in the environment around them

spread Two facing pages in a book

templates Patterns of individual pieces to cut out and assemble

three-dimensional (3-D) Having height, width, and depth

traditional Describes something people have been doing for a long time

volvelles Layered paper disks that turn to line up various sets of data

LEARNING MORE

BOOKS

Ceceri, Kathy. *Paper Inventions* (Make:). Maker Media, 2015.

Hiebert, Helen. *Playing with Paper: Illuminating, Engineering, and Reimagining Paper Art.* Quarry Books, 2013.

Johnson, Pauline. *Creating with Paper: Basic Forms and Variations.* Dover Publications, 2012.

Phillips, Trish, and Ann Montanaro. *Making Pop-Ups & Novelty Cards: A Masterclass in the Art of Paper Engineering.* Lorenz Books, 2016.

WEBSITES

Check out the "Make a Pop-up" and "Explore Pop-ups" pages on pop-up master Robert Sabuda's website:
http://wp.robertsabuda.com

Visit "Instructables" to find templates for papercraft toys and models, or use the ideas to get started on your own creations:
www.instructables.com/howto/papercraft

Take a look at the work of paper engineer David Hawcock, whose paper engineering creations are featured in this book, at:
http://hawcockbooks.co.uk

Go to Renee Jablow's professional website to see examples of projects by someone who works in paper engineering:
www.reneejablow.com

Visit Cybèle Young's website to see her inventive paper creations:
www.cybeleyoung.ca

INDEX